You Breathe In, You Breathe Out
All About Your Lungs

by David A. Adler
Illustrated by Diane Paterson

Franklin Watts

New York   London   Toronto   Sydney

A Discovering Science Book

1991

You breathe in. You breathe out. You are always breathing. You take a breath every three or four seconds.

You breathe in air.

You can't see it but air is all around you. If you wave your hand or a paper fan, you feel a breeze. The breeze is air moving.

The air all around you, the air you breathe, is a mixture. It's a mixture of oxygen, nitrogen, and other gases. You breathe because your body needs the oxygen in air.

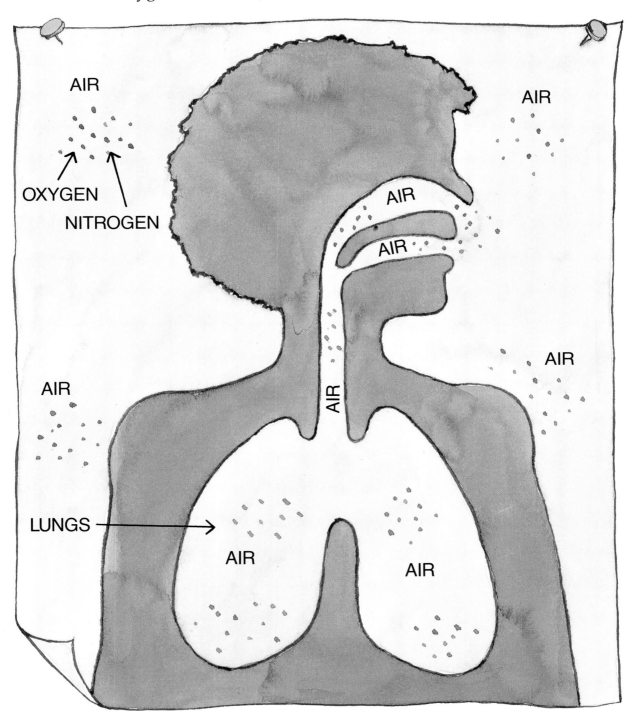

You breathe in. You breathe out.

You usually breathe in through your nose. But sometimes, when you need air quickly, you breathe large gulps of air through your mouth. And sometimes, when you have a cold and your nose is clogged, you also breathe through your mouth.

The air you breathe may be very cold. Before it reaches your lungs it is warmed by the skin inside your nose.

The air might be dirty. In your nose and wind-pipe, also called the **trachea** (*tray*-key-uh), are tiny hairs called **cilia** (*sil*-e-uh). These hairs trap dust and germs before they reach your lungs.

The air you breathe might be dry. In your nose and windpipe there are also **mucous membranes** (*myoo*-kuhs *mem*-brains), which are moist and sticky skin. They wet the air you breathe. They also catch dust and germs.

But the tiny hairs and mucous membranes do not catch everything. That's why sometimes you cough or sneeze. Coughing and sneezing get rid of dust, germs, and other things that may come in through your nose or mouth.

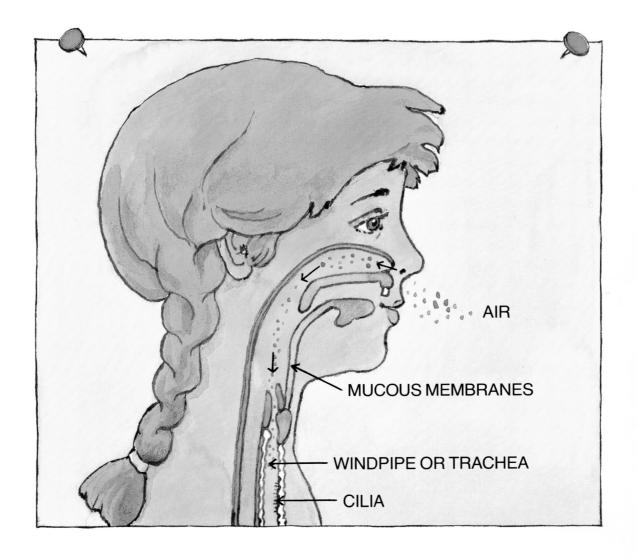

AIR

MUCOUS MEMBRANES

WINDPIPE OR TRACHEA

CILIA

You breathe in. You breathe out.

The air you breathe in passes through your nose or mouth to your **pharynx** (*far*-ingks). Two tubes meet in the pharynx. One is for air. It leads to your lungs. The other is for food. It leads to your stomach. When air comes in through your nose or mouth, it passes through your pharynx to your windpipe (**trachea**).

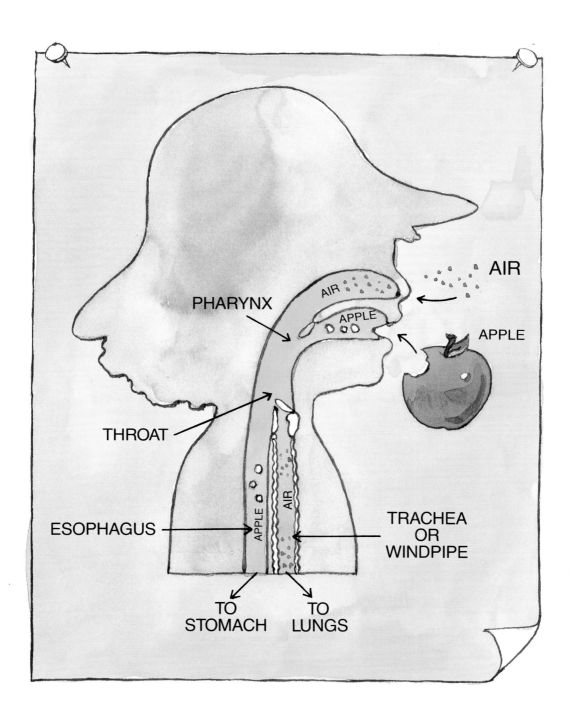

PHARYNX

AIR

AIR

APPLE

APPLE

THROAT

ESOPHAGUS

APPLE

AIR

TRACHEA
OR
WINDPIPE

TO
STOMACH

TO
LUNGS

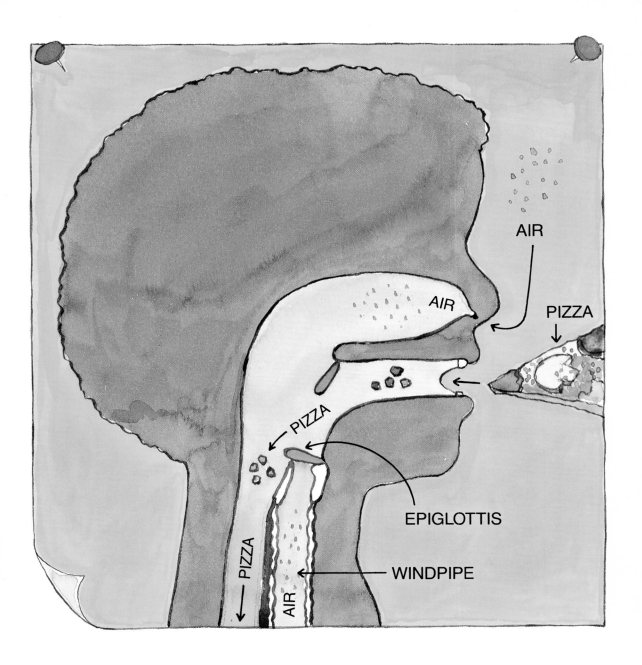

Your windpipe has a small cover, the **epiglottis**
(*ep*-uh-*glot*-tis). It is usually open to let air through.
But when you swallow food it closes. It keeps food
from "going down the wrong pipe." It keeps food out
of your windpipe.

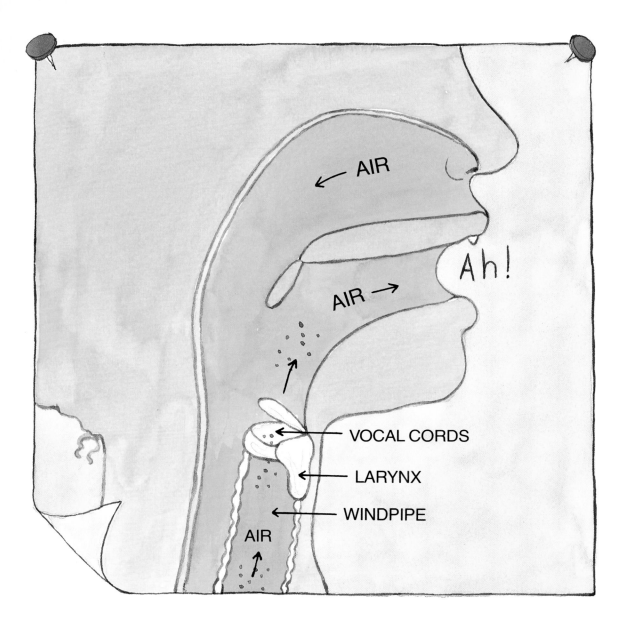

At the very top of your windpipe is your **larynx** (*lar*-ingks), or voice box. In it are two bands of tissue called **vocal cords**. When you breathe, air just passes by these cords. When you speak, air leaving your lungs makes these cords move back and forth very quickly. These movements are called "vibrations" and it's these vibrations that make sounds and words.

Gently touch your neck while you hum or talk.
Can you feel where the vibrations are the strongest?
If you can, you have found your voice box.

Ah!

You breathe in. You breathe out.

The air you breathe in moves through your windpipe. And then it divides. Some of the air goes through a tube to the left and some goes through a tube to the right. These are the **bronchi** (*brong*-key) tubes. Each tube is called a **bronchus** (*brong*-kus).

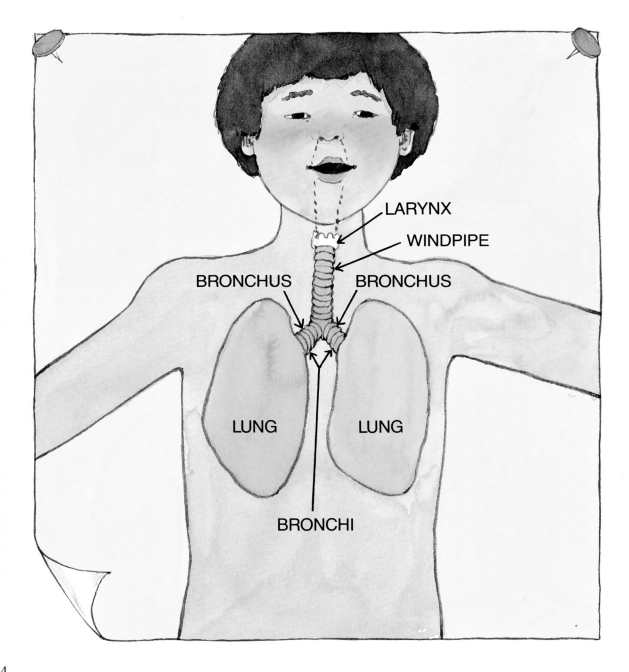

LARYNX

WINDPIPE

BRONCHUS

BRONCHUS

LUNG

LUNG

BRONCHI

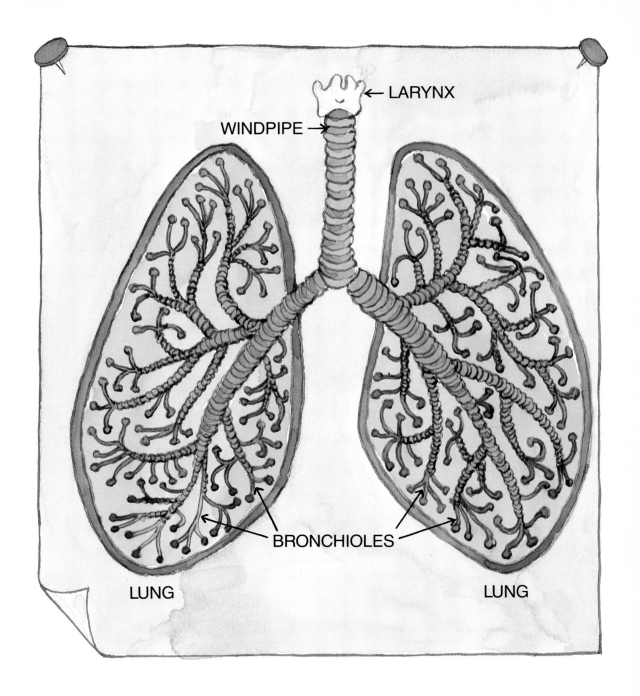

LARYNX

WINDPIPE →

BRONCHIOLES

LUNG   LUNG

Your bronchi lead into your lungs. Inside your
lungs the air passes through these tubes and divides
again and again as it goes through smaller and smaller
tubes called **bronchioles** (*brong* -key-oles).

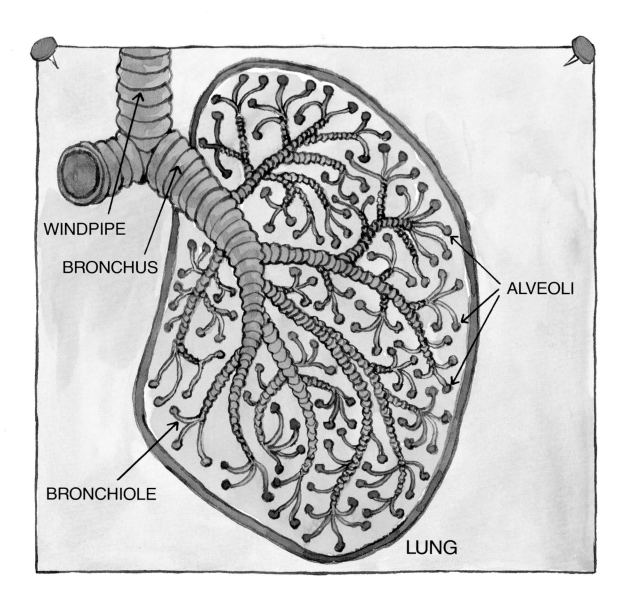

WINDPIPE

BRONCHUS

ALVEOLI

BRONCHIOLE

LUNG

The air you breathe in passes through one tube to the next. Once the air flows through the smallest tubes in your lungs, it passes into tiny sacs of air called **alveoli** (al-*vee*-oh-*lee*). There are millions of these air sacs in each lung.

Each one of these millions of air sacs is covered with tiny tubes carrying blood. These tubes are called **capillaries** (*kap*-uh-ler-ees).

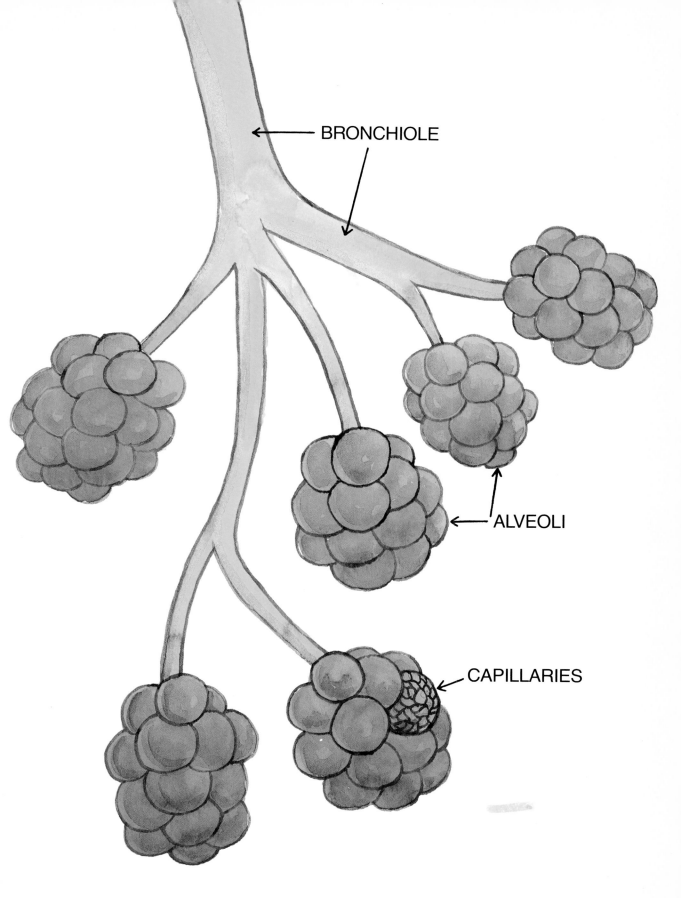

BRONCHIOLE

ALVEOLI

CAPILLARIES

17

A bunch of grapes might help you to understand what happens to the air you breathe. A bunch of grapes has a main stem [bronchi] which leads to smaller stems which lead to even smaller stems [bronchioles]. And the smallest stems lead to the grapes [alveoli].

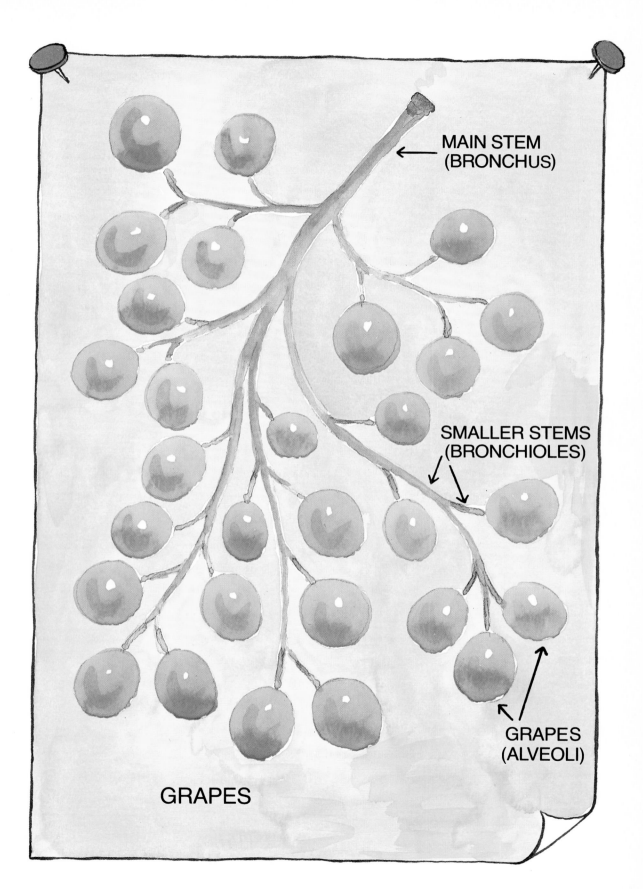

MAIN STEM
(BRONCHUS)

SMALLER STEMS
(BRONCHIOLES)

GRAPES
(ALVEOLI)

GRAPES

You breathe in. You breathe out.

Once the air you breathe in reaches your alveoli, the oxygen in the air passes through the very thin walls of the capillaries and into your blood.

While the capillaries are taking in oxygen from the air, they are also releasing waste air. The waste air, air from which your body has taken oxygen, passes from your capillaries and into your alveoli.

You breathe out the waste air. It passes from your alveoli through your bronchioles and windpipe and out your nose or mouth.

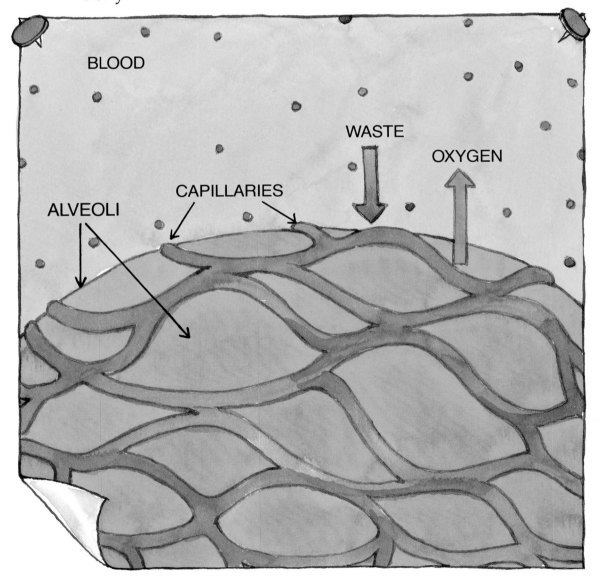

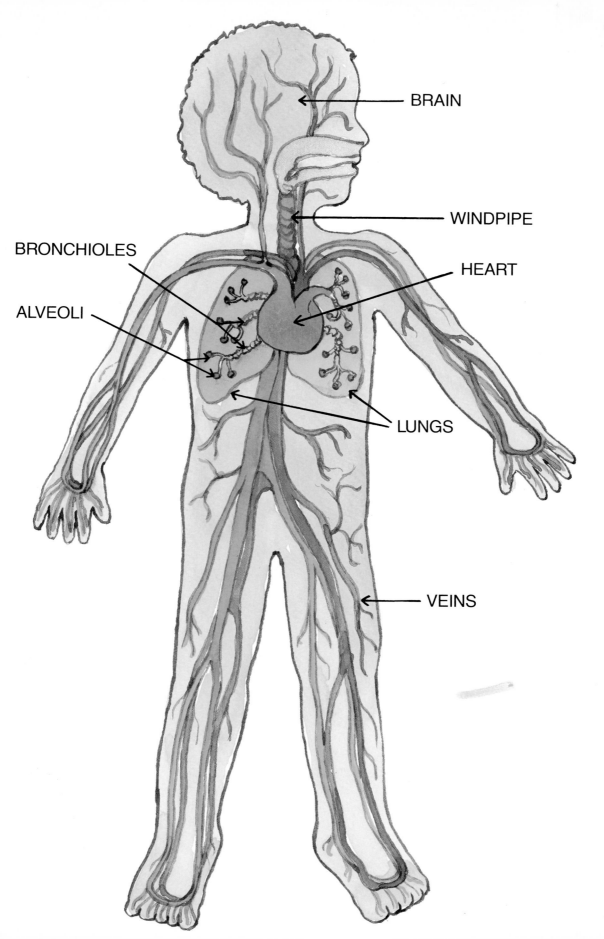

BRAIN

WINDPIPE

BRONCHIOLES

HEART

ALVEOLI

LUNGS

VEINS

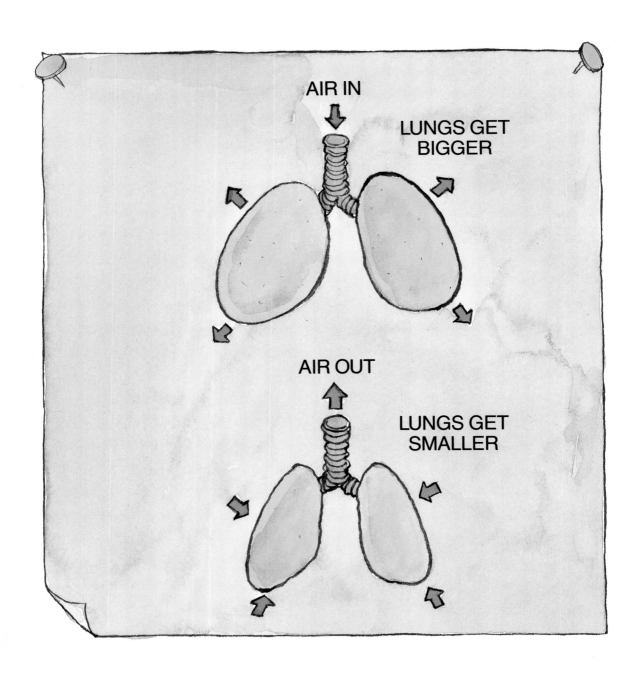

When you breathe in, your lungs fill with air. They get bigger. When you breathe out, your lungs get smaller.

Place your hands on your chest. Take a deep breath. You can feel your chest expand as your lungs fill with air. Now let the air out. Your chest and lungs get smaller.

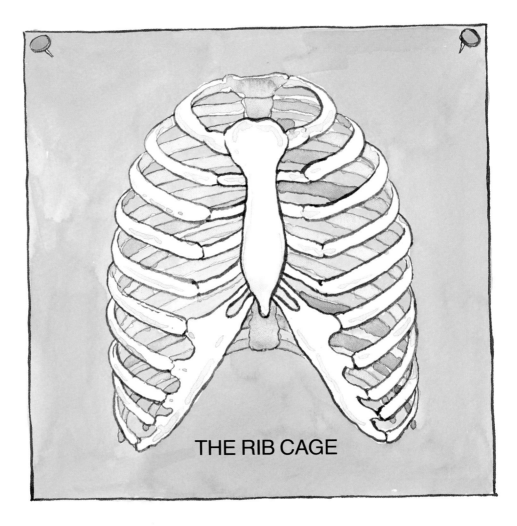

THE RIB CAGE

Your lungs have no muscles. Your lungs need help to get bigger and draw in air and to get smaller and force the air out.

Your lungs are surrounded by ribs, a cage of bones that protects your lungs and heart. Attached to your lower ribs is a large muscle, your **diaphragm** (*die*-uh-*fram*). Every three or four seconds your diaphragm stretches downward and your ribs move outward. This creates extra empty space around your lungs.

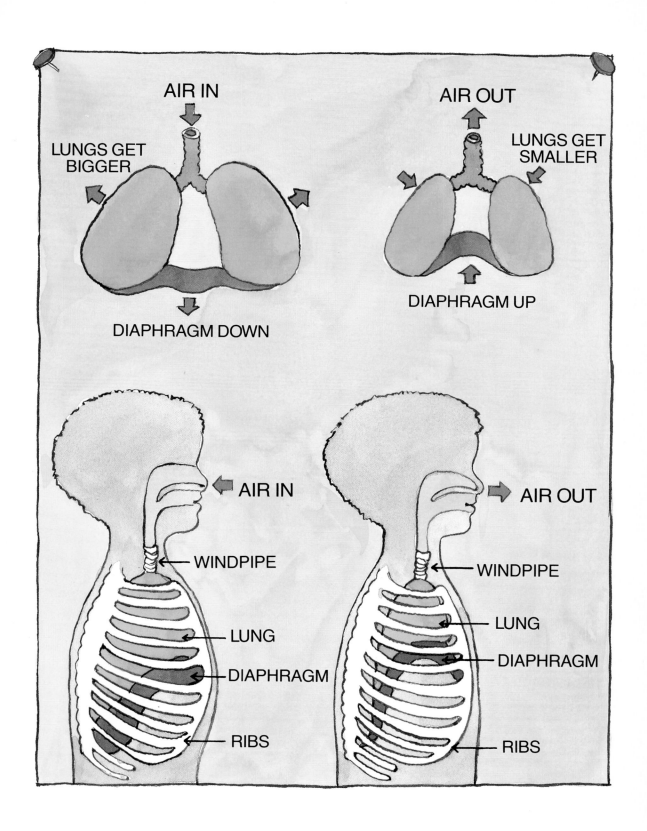

AIR IN

LUNGS GET BIGGER

DIAPHRAGM DOWN

AIR OUT

LUNGS GET SMALLER

DIAPHRAGM UP

AIR IN

WINDPIPE

LUNG

DIAPHRAGM

RIBS

AIR OUT

WINDPIPE

LUNG

DIAPHRAGM

RIBS

25

Air rushes in through your nose or mouth, through your trachea and bronchial tubes, and then fills your alveoli. The movements of your diaphragm and ribs force you to breathe in, to **inhale** air.

When your diaphragm pushes up, your ribs move in and force you to breathe out, to **exhale** air.

Hold your hand close to your mouth and nose. Take a deep breath. As you inhale you can feel the air rushing in. As you exhale you can feel the air going out.

INHALE!

You breathe in. You breathe out.

You don't have to remember to breathe. When your body needs oxygen your brain sends a message to your diaphragm. The message tells your diaphragm to move down and forces your lungs to draw in air.

Things to Do
1. Clean room
2. Do homework
3. Breathe

You breathe in and breathe out thousands of times each day, millions of times each year. While you seldom think about doing it, breathing is a vital part of the whole wonderful process of being alive.

GLOSSARY

Alveoli (al-*vee*-oh-*lee*) Tiny sacs of air in the lungs.

Bronchi (*brong*-key) The two main branches of the trachea.

Bronchioles (*brong*-key-*oles*) Tiny thin-walled airways through which air passes from the bronchi to the alveoli.

Capillaries (*kap*-uh-ler-ees) Tiny blood vessels.

Cilia (*sil*-e-uh) Short, tiny hairs.

Diaphragm (*die*-uh-*fram*) The curved band of muscle and tissue that separates the chest from the abdominal cavity.

Epiglottis (*ep*-uh-*glot*-is) A thin piece of cartilage that covers the trachea during swallowing.

Esophagus (e-*sof*-uh-gus) Also called the food pipe or gullet; it connects the pharynx with the stomach.

Larynx (*lar*-ingks) Also called the voice box; it is the upper part of the trachea and contains the vocal cords.

Mucus (*myoo*-kuhs) The sticky substance which lines the nasal passages and the trachea.

Pharynx (*far*-ingks) Also called the throat; it connects the mouth and nasal passages with the esophagus and trachea.

Trachea (*tray*-key-uh) Also called the windpipe; it is the main trunk of the system of tubes through which air passes to the lungs.

Vocal cords (*vo*-kuhl *kordz*) Two pairs of tissue folds that project into the larynx. Air passing over the vocal cords produces the voice.

Library of Congress Cataloging-In-Publication Data

Adler, David A.
You breathe in, you breathe out: all about your lungs/
by David A. Adler : illustrations by Diane Paterson
p.   cm.—(A Discovering science book)
Summary: Discusses respiration and the lungs, introducing various parts of the respiratory system and explaining how they relate to each other.
ISBN 0-531-10700-0
1. Respiration—Juvenile literature. 2. Lungs—Physiology—Juvenile literature. [1. Respiratory system. 2. Respiration. 3. Lungs.] I. Diane Paterson , ill. II. Title. III. Series· Discovering science (Franklin Watts, inc.)
QP121.A43   1991
612'.2—dc19   88-37835 CIP AC